P9-AGA-707

This rising mOon book belongs to

_____

My Name is gabito

The Life of
Gabriel García Márquez

by **Monica Brown**
Illustrated by **Raúl Colón**

rising moon

Text © 2007 by Monica Brown
Illustrations © 2007 by Raúl Colón
All rights reserved.

This book may not be reproduced in whole or in part, by any means (with the exception of short quotes
for the purpose of review), without permission of the publisher. For information, address Permissions,
Rising Moon, P. O. Box 1389, Flagstaff, Arizona 86002-1389.

www.risingmoonbooks.com

Composed in the United States of America
Printed in China

Edited by Theresa Howell
Designed by David Jenney and Sunny H. Yang

Author's Note
I would like to thank my extraordinary editor, Theresa Howell,
for her vision, her passion, and her many gifts.

Publisher's Note
This book is an independent character study by Monica Brown, Associate Professor of English at
Northern Arizona University in Flagstaff, Arizona. She has not consulted with or had the participation of
Gabriel García Márquez in its preparation and Gabriel García Márquez has not authorized or endorsed
this book. In 2003, Gabriel García Márquez published his memoir, *Living to Tell the Tale* (Knopf),
where he wrote about Lorenzo the Magnificent, ghosts, and the politics and passions that shaped his
childhood. The author referred to this memoir and a plentitude of reference works for
factual background information in preparing this character study for children.

FIRST ENGLISH IMPRESSION 2007
ISBN 13: 978-0-87358-934-5 (HC)
ISBN 10: 0-87358-934-3 (HC)

FIRST ENGLISH IMPRESSION 2007
ISBN 13: 978-0-87358-949-9 (SC)
ISBN 10: 0-87358-949-1 (SC)

07   08   09   10   11   5   4   3   2   1

Library of Congress Cataloging-in-Publication Data

Brown, Monica, 1969-
My name is Gabito : the life of Gabriel García Márquez / by Monica Brown.
p. cm.
ISBN-13: 978-0-87358-934-5 (hardcover)
ISBN-10: 0-87358-934-3 (hardcover)
1. García Márquez, Gabriel, 1928---Juvenile literature. 2. Authors, Colombian--20th century--
Biography--Juvenile literature. I. Title.
PQ8180.17.A73Z613 2007
863'.64--dc22
[B]
2007008950

To Jeff Berglund

—M. B.

For Zeke, a long-lost friend

—R. C.

Can you imagine a shipwrecked sailor living on
air and seaweed for eight days?

Can you imagine a trail of yellow butterflies
fluttering their wings to songs of love?

Can you imagine gold and silver fish
swimming in air?

Can you imagine?

Once, there was a little boy named Gabito who could. This little boy would become one of the greatest storytellers of all time.

Gabito was born in the magical town of Aracataca, Colombia, and his imagination was just as big and great and wild as the thickest jungles and highest mountaintops of Colombia.

To Gabito, the world was a magical place. He grew up in a little house with his big family and, according to his grandmother, a strange and mysterious ghost. Sometimes little Gabito would imagine the ghostlady gliding through his house and rocking the empty rocking chair in the family room.
Back and forth. Back and forth.

Gabito never sat in that rocking chair because he didn't want to squish the ghost.

Gabito's imagination was big.

Gabito also lived with an amazing 100-year-old talking parrot named Lorenzo the Magnificent. Lorenzo would make up stories of his own, just like Gabito. And sometimes his stories turned out to be true!

One day Gabito listened to Lorenzo tell a story about a big, angry bull getting loose. Imagine his surprise when a big, angry bull ran right through his kitchen! Maybe, thought Gabito, Lorenzo the Magnificent had magical powers.

Gabito's imagination was wild.

Gabito's favorite person in the whole world was his grandfather Nicolas, who had a giant dictionary filled with many amazing words. From this dictionary, Gabito learned that magic is not just for witches, that gypsies are wanderers with a taste for adventure, and that words can be big and great and wild, too.

The more words Gabito learned, the more stories he told.

Each day after breakfast, Gabito and his grandfather put on matching Scotch plaid hats and walked through the town of Aracataca, holding hands and smelling the jasmine flowers. The two of them would walk happily towards the café, where they met his grandfather's friends for lunch. His grandfather always let him dip his hands into the pitcher of water and lift out the cold and crunchy ice cubes.

The more people Gabito met, the more stories he told.

Sometimes Gabito and his grandfather walked past
the big banana plantation at the edge of town. He saw
how hard the people on the banana plantation worked
picking fruit. Even to little Gabito, it didn't seem fair
that those who worked so hard were so poor, and this
made Gabito sad. He tried to imagine a world where no
one was poor and where everyone could sit with their
grandfathers under the shade of a tree, holding hands
and crunching ice.

The more things Gabito saw, the more stories he told.

Under the hot sun, Gabito grew tall. He learned that ghosts were real, that parrots sometimes speak the truth, and that not everything, even in this magical world, is fair. Most importantly he learned that he loved stories. He loved hearing them, reading them, telling them, and writing them. He loved creating worlds where the impossible was possible, where dreams were true, and where people could float and fly.

The more stories he wrote, the more he wanted to write.

When Gabito grew up he wrote the most exciting stories in the world. His stories were magical and amazing, but just as real as you or me.

Can you imagine what kind of stories Gabito told?

Close your eyes and see.

Can you imagine?

Can you imagine a man with enormous wings falling from the sky?

Can you imagine the most beautiful woman in the world?

Can you imagine?

Can you imagine flying through the air on a magic carpet?

If these stories sound magical it is because they are. And they were written by the boy called Gabito, who grew up to be Gabriel García Márquez, the great storyteller, read by millions, loved by all. But Gabito never forgot the parrot and the bull, the jasmine flowers and the banana workers, and the dictionary full of wonderful words.

People on all seven continents read his stories and love them and discover just how magical—and big and great and wild—the world can be.

Gabriel García Márquez

Gabriel García Márquez has a gift. He is a storyteller. On March 6, 1928, Gabriel, nicknamed Gabito, was born in Aracataca, a town in northern Colombia. Gabito was raised by his grandparents in a house filled with brothers, sisters, aunts, cousins, and a 100-year-old parrot named Lorenzo the Magnificent. Gabito learned a great deal from his grandfather and his grandmother, who told many stories themselves.

Over the years, Gabito worked as a journalist and a novelist. He lived in Europe, the United States, and Mexico, among other places. In 1958 he married his childhood sweetheart, Mercedes Bacha Pardo, and they had two sons, Rodrigo and Gonzalo.

Gabito's early life was also shaped by the struggles of the poor banana workers. He believed in the workers' fight for fairness. Even when Gabito became one of the most famous writers in the world, he never forgot the workers, and their stories made their way into his novels and his life.

Gabriel García Márquez has written over thirty books, including *Love in the Time of Cholera* (1988), *Living to Tell the Tale* (2003), and his most brilliant novel, *One Hundred Years of Solitude* (1967). In 1982 he was awarded the Nobel Prize for Literature. His stories are celebrated all over the world. He writes most often about Colombia, sharing stories of people and places that are both magical and real. He lives in Mexico City, where his genius for storytelling continues to be a gift to us all.

MONICA BROWN is an award-winning writer of multicultural picture books. Her first book won the 2005 Américas Award for Children's Literature. Inspired by her heritage, Monica Brown continues to write magical books for children. She lives in Flagstaff, Arizona, with her husband, Jeff, and two daughters. Find out more about Monica Brown at www.monicabrown.net.

RAÚL COLÓN was born in New York City, and moved with his parents to Caguas, Puerto Rico, where he studied commercial art. In 1988 the artist settled with his family back in New York City and began a freelance career. Today, Raúl is a versatile and acclaimed illustrator whose work has appeared in important national publications such as *The New York Times* and *Time Magazine*. Raúl completes his work for his grownup clients while continually winning acclaim for his children's picture books.